5TO

ACPL ITEM
DISCARDED
808.8
SING
P9-EDX-852

SING FREEDOM!

Judith Nicholls was born into a small farming community in Lincolnshire but spent her schooldays in a seaside town on the east coast. After various travels she settled with her husband and three children in Wiltshire, where she still lives. Although her first remembered poem was written at the age of seven, she taught for some years before deciding to concentrate more seriously on her own writing and her work as a Writer in Schools.

by the same author

MAGIC MIRROR
and other poems for children

MIDNIGHT FOREST
and other poems

DRAGONSFIRE
and other poems

POPCORN PIE
(Mary Glasgow Publications)

HIGGLEDY-HUMBUG
(Mary Glasgow Publications)

edited by Judith Nicholls

WORDSPELLS

WHAT ON EARTH . . . ?
Poems with a Conservation Theme

SING FREEDOM!

An anthology of poems

compiled by Judith Nicholls

faber and faber
LONDON · BOSTON

First published in Great Britain in 1991
by Faber and Faber Limited
3 Queen Square London WC1N 3AU

Photoset by Wilmaset Birkenhead Wirral
Printed in Great Britain by
Clays Ltd St Ives plc

A CIP record for this book
is available from the British Library

ISBN: 0 571 16513 3
0 571 16514 1 (Pbk)

10 9 8 7 6 5 4 3 2 1

I am writing to inform you that after six years, four months, seventeen days in prison, I am free. I walked out of the prison gate with my shoulders unbent, my head unbowed. I can touch the green leaves of the trees. I can smell the sweet scent of flowers. I can share smiles and laughter with the women and children.

Surely there is nothing so sweet, so beautiful, so precious as freedom and liberty.

Professor Maina Wa Kinyatti,
former prisoner of conscience, Kenya.

This book is for all those who have been silenced,
and for those who speak for them.

Contents

Introduction

'But we don't want all those things,' said an old bear. 'We want to be free.'

C. S. Lewis

The year I was born Roosevelt was looking forward to a world founded upon four essential freedoms: freedom of speech and expression, freedom for every person to worship God in his own way, freedom from want, freedom from fear. Fifty years on, world events continue dramatically to show how much remains to be done.

Our awareness of freedom is most sharply defined by its loss. For thirty years Amnesty International has worked throughout the world on behalf of individuals who have unjustly suffered that loss; this anthology is for them.

Choosing the poems has been particularly difficult. When I first initiated this project I searched many books for 'freedom' poems, as well as writing to many individual poets. Later, a small notice in a Sunday newspaper brought in over 2000 further poems! Many writers wrote warmly supporting AI and offering their fees too towards the organization, should their work be used. I thank them and apologize that we could not include more of their poems. Few compilers can hope to escape accusations of omission but I hope that this selection will be enjoyed as a *starting point* into the literature of freedom.

Judith Nicholls
February, 1991

SING FREEDOM!

from Crossing

Free me as free are the birds of the wilds, the wanderers
of unseen paths.
Free me as free are the deluge of rain, and the storm
that shakes its locks and rushes on to its unknown
end.
Free me as free is the forest fire, as is the thunder that
laughs aloud and hurls defiance to darkness.

Rabindranath Tagore

from Liberty

But what is Freedom? Rightly understood,
A universal licence to be good.

Hartley Coleridge (1796–1849)

Lines translated from Euripides

This is true liberty when freeborn men
Having to advise the public may speak free,
Which he who can, and will, deserves high praise
Who neither can nor will, may hold his peace;
What can be juster in a state than this?

John Milton (1608–1674)

from The Bruce

Ah! fredome is a noble thing!
Fredome mayse man to haiff liking.

John Barbour (1316–1395)

'Tell me now'

'Tell me now, what should a man want
But to sit alone, sipping his cup of wine?'
I should like to have visitors come and discuss philosophy
And not to have the tax-collector coming to collect taxes;
My three sons married into good families
And my five daughters wedded to steady husbands.
Then I could jog through a happy five-score years
And, at the end, need no Paradise.

Wang Chi (AD 584–644) (translated by Arthur Waley)

from Table Talk

Freedom has a thousand charms to show,
That slaves, howe'er contented, never know.

William Cowper (1731–1800)

'When the sun rises'

When the sun rises, I go to work,
When the sun goes down, I take my rest,
I dig the well from which I drink,
I farm the soil that yields my food,
I share creation, Kings can do no more.

Anon (Chinese, 2500 BC)

Two Old Black Men on a Leicester Square Park Bench

What do you dream of you
old black men sitting
on park benches staunchly
wrapped up in scarves
and coats of silence
eyes far away from the cold
grey and strutting
pigeon
ashy fingers trembling
(though it's said that the old
hardly ever feel the cold)

do you dream revolutions
you could have forged
or mourn
some sunfull woman you
might have known a
hibiscus flower
ghost memories of desire

O it's easy
to rainbow the past
after all the letters from
home spoke of hardships

and the sun was traded long ago

Grace Nichols

The Rebel

When everybody has short hair,
The rebel lets his hair grow long.

When everybody has long hair,
The rebel cuts his hair short.

When everybody talks during the lesson,
The rebel doesn't say a word.

When nobody talks during the lesson,
The rebel creates a disturbance.

When everybody wears a uniform,
The rebel dresses in fantastic clothes.

When everybody wears fantastic clothes,
The rebel dresses soberly.

In the company of dog lovers,
The rebel expresses a preference for cats.

In the company of cat lovers,
The rebel puts in a good word for dogs.

When everybody is praising the sun,
The rebel remarks on the need for rain.

When everybody is greeting the rain,
The rebel regrets the absence of sun.

When everybody goes to the meeting,
The rebel stays at home and reads a book.

When everybody stays at home and reads a book,
The rebel goes to the meeting.

When everybody says, Yes please,
The rebel says, No thank you.

When everybody says, No thank you,
The rebel says, Yes please.

It is very good that we have rebels.
You may not find it very good to be one.

D. J. Enright

Didactica Nova

How many fingers have you got on one hand?
Five, replied the child.
So, how many do five and five make?
Eleven, comes the answer.
Can you blame me for getting cross with you?
Didn't I say count?
Why can't you understand
And answer like all the rest!
What if everyone answered like that?
What would happen if nobody understood?
How many fingers have you got on one hand?
Five, replied the child.
Well, how many on two hands?
Eleven, comes the answer.
The blows fall. On the hand with five fingers,
On the hand
    with six.

Grete Tartler (translated by Andrea Deletant and Brenda Walker)

'Everything is for our own good'

Everything is for our own good.
Road sweepers who stop us falling
on banana skins.
The card you clock in with.
The heavenly view of the park in autumn.
The anadin, the valium, the ethic and rhetoric.
The hotel receptionist, who carefully checks
that we don't have different names (Wink! Wink!)
that we don't have different addresses (Nudge! Nudge!)
  the laws, decrees,
and their amendments.
Everything is for our own good.
The (ancient) inscriptions HIC FUIT . . .
and the (modern) imperatives: don't walk on the grass,
don't slam the door, don't leave me yet. Don't . . .
  purely and simply
carefully and gently with our lives
so that in no way can we go off the rails,
when
everything is for our own good:
the (verbal) reprimand of friends
the (written) reprimand of public opinion
the increased salary, services of small cooperatives
messengers of love, the agony columns.
Hearts, lungs and brain.
God, how ashamed I've become.
Everything's for our own good.
Benevolent Funds and X rays,
blood from the O Group,
and radium, radium, radium.

Daniela Crăsnaru (translated by Andrea Deletant and Brenda Walker)

The Council of the Gods

Lay no blame. Have pity.
Put your fingers in the wounds of the committee.

They never reached your item.
Disputing Item One *ad infinitum*.

Lay no blame. Be tender.
The retrospective start of the agenda

Was all they managed treating.
Consider, pray, the feeling of the meeting.

(They felt awful.) Not surprising
They never came to matters not arising

From Matters Arising:

> *Who took the chair when the standing committee last sat?*
> *Who kept the minutes for hours and hours and hours?*
> *Who tabled the motion,*
> *Who motioned the table*
> *Whereat*
> *The standing committee*
> *Sat?*

Have pity.
Put your fingers in the wounds of the committee.

The gods have not been sleeping.
All night they sat, in grief and boredom, weeping.

Kit Wright

The Unknown Citizen

(To JS/07/M/378
This Marble Monument
Is Erected by the State)

He was found by the Bureau of Statistics to be
One against whom there was no official complaint,
And all the reports on his conduct agree
That, in the modern sense of an old-fashioned word, he was a saint,
For in everything he did he served the Greater Community.
Except for the War till the day he retired
He worked in a factory and never got fired,
But satisfied his employers, Fudge Motors Inc.
Yet he wasn't a scab or odd in his views,
For his Union reports that he paid his dues,
(Our report on his Union shows it was sound)
And our Social Psychology workers found
That he was popular with his mates and liked a drink.
The Press are convinced that he bought a paper every day
And that his reactions to advertisements were normal in
  every way.
Policies taken out in his name prove that he was fully insured,
And his Health-card shows he was once in hospital but left it cured.
Both Producers Research and High-Grade Living declare
He was fully sensible to the advantages of the Instalment Plan
And had everything necessary to the Modern Man,
A phonograph, a radio, a car and a frigidaire.
Our researchers into Public Opinion are content
That he held the proper opinions for the time of year;
When there was peace, he was for peace; when there was war,
  he went.
He was married and added five children to the population,
Which our Eugenist says was the right number for a parent of
  his generation,
And our teachers report that he never interfered with their
  education.
Was he free? Was he happy? The question is absurd:
Had anything been wrong, we should certainly have heard.

W. H. Auden

Domestic policy

The state he thought he could ignore

Until it
Walked in
His front
Door . . .

David Heidenstam

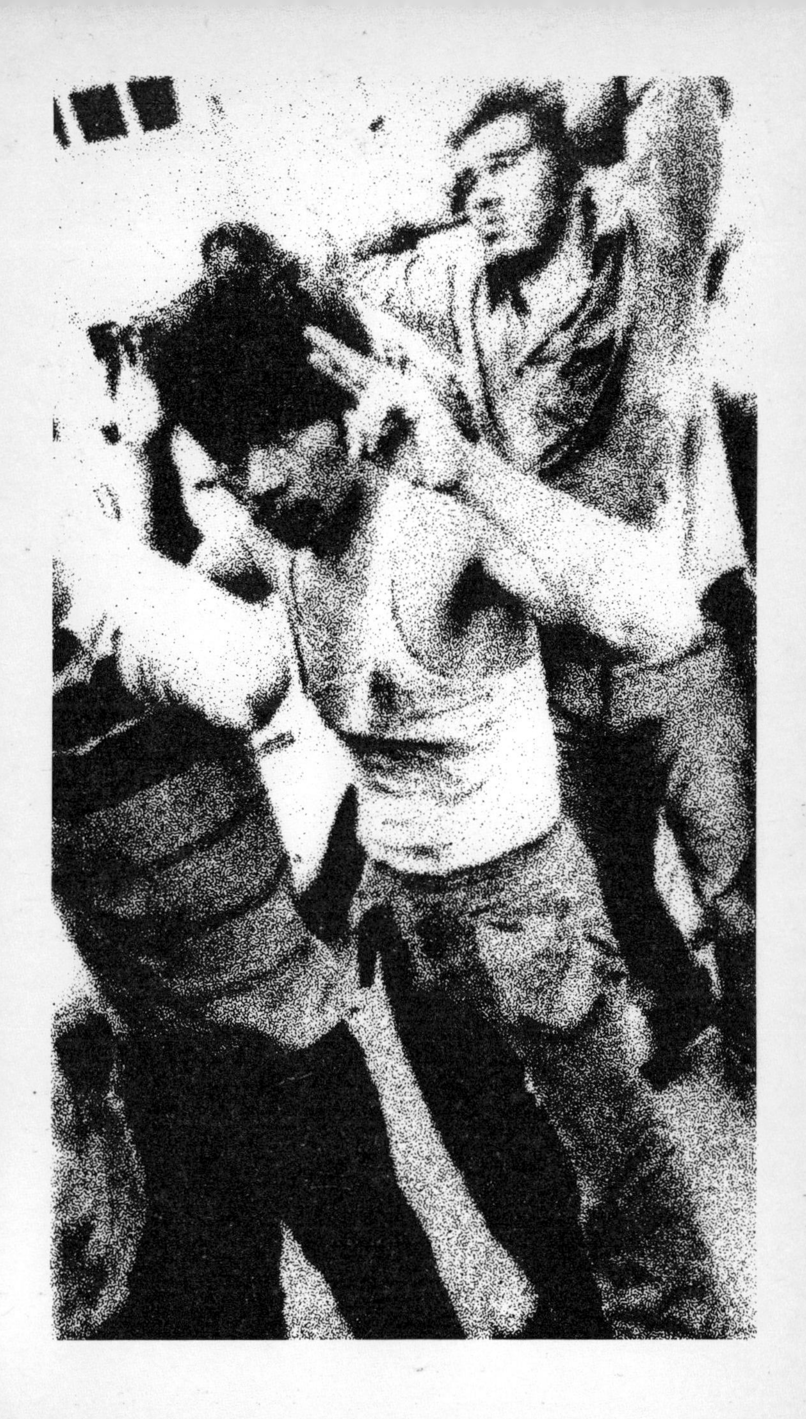

Dictator

From a strange land among the hills, the tall man
Came; who was a cobbler and a rebel at the start
Till he saw power ahead and keenly fought
To seize it; crushed out his comrades then.
His brittle eyes could well outstare the eagle
And the young followed him with cheers and praise
Until, at last, all that they knew – his nights, his days,
His deeds and face were parcel of a fable.

Now in the neat white house that is his home
He rules the flowers and birds just like a king,
And, Napoleon by the sundial, sees his fame
Spread through the garden to the heap of dung;
'All that I do is history,' he loudly cries
Seeing in his shadow his romantic size.

Ruthven Todd

Decree

It has been decided
that certain incontrovertible truths
which have been . . .

> the bulwark of our freedoms
> sheet anchor of our constitution
> backbone of our laws
> cornerstone of our institutions
> buttress of our defence
> foundation of our education system
> warp and weft of our social life
> source of all our achievements in science and technology
> rallying cry for our leaders
> spur to our sportsmen who dominate the world
> comfort to the widows of our slaughtered soldiers
> inspiration to our painters and musicians
> . . . and most of our poets, dramatists and novelists
> linchpin of our triumphant revolution
> climax of our glorious history
> and pivot of our civilisation . . .

are no longer incontrovertible
and will be replaced by
a new incontrovertible truth
that shall be . . .

> the sheet anchor of our new constitution
> bulwark of our developing freedoms
> backbone of our laws
> cornerstone, linchpin, pivot, focal point of the nation

and make us the envy of the world.

Tony Sims

The Watch-Dogs

Every day, the watch-dogs raise their muzzles
A little higher

They become more sensitive,
Reliable, subtle,
As the century ticks away

The watch-dogs
Do not bear looking at
Nor thinking of

They are very susceptible
To tremors and disaffection –
Do not upset them

They can hear grass growing
And the embryo quick in the womb

How long they will tolerate this
We do not know

Elma Mitchell

A Constable Calls

His bicycle stood at the window-sill,
The rubber cowl of a mud-splasher
Skirting the front mudguard,
Its fat black handlegrips

Heating in sunlight, the 'spud'
Of the dynamo gleaming and cocked back,
The pedal treads hanging relieved
Of the boot of the law.

His cap was upside down
On the floor, next his chair.
The line of its pressure ran like a bevel
In his slightly sweating hair.

He had unstrapped
The heavy ledger, and my father
Was making tillage returns
In acres, roods, and perches.

Arithmetic and fear.
I sat staring at the polished holster
With its buttoned flap, the braid cord
Looped into the revolver butt.

'Any other root crops?
Mangolds? Marrowstems? Anything like that?'
'No.' But was there not a line
Of turnips where the seed ran out

In the potato field? I assumed
Small guilts and sat
Imagining the black hole in the barracks.
He stood up, shifted the baton-case

Further round on his belt,
Closed the domesday book,
Fitted his cap back with two hands,
And looked at me as he said goodbye.

A shadow bobbed in the window.
He was snapping the carrier spring
Over the ledger. His boot pushed off
And the bicycle ticked, ticked, ticked.

Seamus Heaney

Voice of Authority

I'll tell you what truth is, confided Pilate,
And somehow we could tell he wasn't jesting,
Quite plain to those who care to make the effort –
Not much to do with beauty or anything
Like that, nor matching argument to fact,
But something simple to get hold of, yet so
Beneficial in overall effect
It's all on earth you ever need to know.
The truth you see is what I say it is,
No more, and though some awkward dissidents
Kick up a fuss and want it otherwise
They soon come round to good old commonsense
So spellbound are they by the symmetries
Of half-truths and the sorcery of lies.

Tony Sims

The Hand That Signed the Paper

The hand that signed the paper felled a city;
Five sovereign fingers taxed the breath,
Doubled the globe of dead and halved a country;
These five kings did a king to death.

The mighty hand leads to a sloping shoulder,
The finger joints are cramped with chalk;
A goose's quill has put an end to murder
That put an end to talk.

The hand that signed the treaty bred a fever,
And famine grew, and locusts came;
Great is the hand that holds dominion over
Man by a scribbled name.

The five kings count the dead but do not soften
The crusted wound nor stroke the brow;
A hand rules pity as a hand rules heaven;
Hands have no tears to flow.

Dylan Thomas

Open Your Arms

in our country
death starts
with the name of a loved one

we are dragged across squares
on our hands
and knees

a friend
raises his gun
the darkness is vast around here

then women
gather their heroes
in their arms

Mevlut Ceylan

from Threnodia Augustalis

Freedom which in no other land will thrive,
Freedom an English subject's sole prerogative.

John Dryden (1631–1700)

Britons Never Shall Be Slaves

Henry Drake still at school sees
His father, put away for
Misbehaviour, wave goodbye.
He cries.

A teenager before the
Word is born, the Army claims
Him for the country's fight for
Freedom.

Benghazi – weather sunny,
Plenty grub; that's new. Payment
Too. Peace intervenes; home to
Blighty.

Better off by one new suit
He's free to find a job, low
Pay, and a girlfriend, Ann, keen
To save.

Romance falls through, but there's his
Cycling, gardening, fishing,
Same boring job, same low wage,
But free.

At forty-four Henry Drake
Is made redundant. 'Sorry . . .
Years . . . cut backs, but we . . . thanks for . . .'
He's free

To care for mother, ailing
Fast. He does his best; she dies
At eighty-two, leaving him
Free to

Stare awhile; at least he's kept
Some hair; he'll join a . . . make new . . .
But Englishmen of Henry's
Station

Unprivileged, no decent
Education, find themselves
Ditched by a freedom loving
Nation.

Helen Heslop

The Ideal State

To be warm
to be fed
with a roof
overhead
and a bed
when it's late
is all
that's required
of the
Ideal State.

Ann Bonner

The Election

They tell me today is important . . .
The first free election occurring
After twenty-nine years; that's more
Than my whole lifetime, and now
Everyone must vote or be fined
(Though having nothing, what could they take?)
Since we are uneducated, simple folk,
Our mayor (and employer), Dom Felipe,
Caring for us as he always does,
He had his servants set up
A feast in the square last night,
With food, drink, and dancing
To Zé Manuel's Rhythm Kings.
Not up to much, of course . . .
An old guitar, the wheezing concertina,
And Grandpa Nuno's erratic drum-beat . . .
Still, we enjoyed the old dances and songs.
And then Dom Felipe, bless him,
He stood up with the voting form
To show us what to do, us being stupid.
The form had pictures of the people,
But without television or newspapers,
We didn't know who they were.
We thought they must all be clever,
So it wouldn't matter who won,
But Dom Felipe said to make an X
Against the bottom picture.
We didn't object; the man looked rich
And very smooth, with a big smile.
I liked the look of the first picture . . .
He seemed like a working-man, plain,
Concerned, straight and honest,
But Dom Felipe knows best, of course.
Anyway, our own ideas would be stupid,
And if our man wins, Dom Felipe
Has promised us a bonus next week.

Elizabeth Hillman

In 1989 Brazil held its first free Presidential elections for twenty-nine years, and some people took up to nine days travelling to and from the nearest town to vote. But many non-lettered voters inadvertently voted for candidates they had not intended to support, due to lack of guidance.

Homage to a Government

Next year we are to bring the soldiers home
For lack of money, and it is all right.
Places they guarded, or kept orderly,
Must guard themselves, and keep themselves orderly.
We want the money for ourselves at home
Instead of working. And this is all right.

It's hard to say who wanted it to happen,
But now it's been decided nobody minds.
The places are a long way off, not here,
Which is all right, and from what we hear
The soldiers there only made trouble happen.
Next year we shall be easier in our minds.

Next year we shall be living in a country
That brought its soldiers home for lack of money.
The statues will be standing in the same
Tree-muffled squares, and look nearly the same.
Our children will not know it's a different country.
All we can hope to leave them now is money.

Philip Larkin

The Angry Man

The other day I chanced to meet
An angry man upon the street –
A man of wrath, a man of war,
A man who truculently bore
Over his shoulder, like a lance,
A banner labelled 'Tolerance'.

And when I asked him why he strode
Thus scowling down the human road,
Scowling, he answered, 'I am he
Who champions total liberty –
Intolerance being, ma'am, a state
No tolerant man can tolerate.

'When I meet rogues,' he cried, 'who choose
To cherish oppositional views,
Lady, like this, and in this manner,
I lay about them with my banner
Till they cry mercy, ma'am.' His blows
Rained proudly on prospective foes.

Fearful, I turned and left him there
Still muttering, as he thrashed the air,
'Let the Intolerant beware!'

Phyllis McGinley

Guns for the Boys

The big man with the gun said,
'I'm here to protect you.'
So he kicked me in the groin,
To show everyone his strength.

The small man with the gun said,
'I'm here to protect you.'
So he burned the factory where I worked,
In case there was a sniper
On the roof.

The dark man with the gun said,
'I'm here to protect you.'
So he knocked down my house,
To get a clear field of fire.

Then the three men with their guns
Lined up and shot me.
'You're easier to protect
When you're dead,'
They said.

Michael Brophy

History Lesson

First, one
in the crowd puts the eye on you –
a nod to number two

who gets the message
and flips back something side-
long, something snide

that everybody hears
but you. Soon three or four
are in it. They'll make sure

you catch the steel
glint of the snigger they wear
like a badge. And there

come five or six
together, casual, shouldering in
around you with a single grin

and nothing you say
seems to reach them at all.
The badmouthings they call

mean only this:
they want to scratch. You are the itch.
Wally. Wimp. Slag. Echoes: *Witch!*

Nigger! Yid!
All you hear is silence lumbered
shut. And the ten or the hundred

looking on
look on. They are learning not to see.
The bell rings, too late. Already

this is history.

Philip Gross

Ballad of the Paper Soldier

A soldier lived upon this earth,
handsome he grew bolder,
but he was a child's toy from birth,
he was a paper soldier.

The world it wanted changing –
happiness to his order,
but he hung on a puppet string,
he was a paper soldier.

He would be happy in fire and smoke
to die for you twice over,
but you fussed over him and spoke:
'You are a paper soldier.'

He cursed his worldly fate
not thirsting for the quiet life
and begged and begged for the fiery state
forgot his paper life.

The fire? Well go, well off you go,
and he walked off the bolder,
And then he burnt in a puff and blow,
he was a paper soldier.

Bulat Okudzhava (translated by Richard McKane)

Thoughts in the Park

I don't have
any money,
the government
takes it all

(soft gossamers
of spring move
silently through the
misty air of the
park as I sit)

I don't have any
freedom, my employer
takes it all

(progressive sun rays
fall, gently bathing
the rising grass
with ultraviolet)

I am everybody,
I have everybody's
problems, I am
the people but

(the soft soil around
my body takes my
mind from its polluted
world of super-giant
factories and)

I think I'll leave
the revolution
until tomorrow.

Robin Mellor

An Appointment

Being out of heart with government
I took a broken root to fling
Where the proud, wayward squirrel went,
Taking delight that he could spring;
And he, with that low whinnying sound
That is like laughter, sprang again
And so to the other tree at a bound.
Nor the tame will, nor timid brain,
Nor heavy knitting of the brow
Bred that fierce tooth and cleanly limb
And threw him up to laugh on the bough;
No government appointed him.

W. B. Yeats

The Democratic Judge

In Los Angeles, before the judge who examines people
Trying to become citizens of the United States
Came an Italian restaurant keeper. After grave preparations
Hindered, though, by his ignorance of the new language
In the test he replied to the question:
What is the 8th Amendment? falteringly:
1492. Since the law demands that applicants know the
language
He was refused. Returning
After three months spent on further studies
Yet hindered still by ignorance of the new language
He was confronted this time with the question: Who was
The victorious general in the Civil War? His answer was:
1492. (Given amiably, in a loud voice.) Sent away again
And returning a third time, he answered
A third question: For how long a term are our Presidents
elected?
Once more with: 1492. Now
The judge, who liked the man, realized that he could not
Learn the new language, asked him
How he earned his living and was told: by hard work.
And so
At his fourth appearance the judge gave him the question:
When
Was America discovered? And on the strength of his
correctly answering
1492, he was granted his citizenship.

Bertolt Brecht (translated by Michael Hamburger)

Lord of Himself

How happy is he born or taught
  Who serveth not another's will;
Whose armour is his honest thought,
  And simple truth his highest skill;

Whose passions not his masters are;
  Whose soul is still prepared for death –
Not tied unto the world with care
  Of prince's ear or vulgar breath;

Who hath his ear from rumours freed;
  Whose conscience is his strong retreat;
Whose state can neither flatterers feed,
  Nor ruin make oppressors great;

Who envies none whom chance doth raise,
  Or vice; who never understood
How deepest wounds are given with praise,
  Nor rules of state but rules of good;

Who God doth late and early pray
  More of his grace than gifts to lend,
And entertains the harmless day
  With a well-chosen book or friend –

This man is free from servile bands
  Of hope to rise or fear to fall:
Lord of himself, though not of lands,
  And, having nothing, yet hath all.

Sir Henry Wotton (1568–1639)

Not Quite Social

Some of you will be glad I did what I did,
And the rest won't want to punish me too severely
For finding a thing to do that though not forbid
Yet wasn't enjoined and wasn't expected, clearly.

To punish me overcruelly wouldn't be right
For merely giving you once more gentle proof
That the city's hold on a man is no more tight
Than when its walls rose higher than any roof.

You may taunt me with not being able to flee the earth.
You have me there, but loosely, as I would be held.
The way of understanding is partly mirth.
I would not be taken as ever having rebelled.

And anyone is free to condemn me to death –
If he leaves it to nature to carry out the sentence.
I shall will to the common stock of air my breath
And pay a death tax of fairly polite repentance.

Robert Frost

In the Hotel

What is more frightening than a door,
Sealed, with a rug over it?
What lies behind? The Angel Mary,
Or a traitor with a hatchet?

Even when talking, it is not possible
To tear your troubled gaze away
From that intricate pattern – if you look
Hard, you might see something.

How can the simple hotel guest
Fail to be puzzled by
The chaotic muddle of
Tower, turret, parapet?

Everything here encourages
Distrust – I draw the rug aside –
The draught that flows from the door
Suggests a long, long passage behind.

There is no chink in it, no knob.
A slight breeze comes from underneath.
Kafka has taught us all about
Such things – we know it by heart.

If it were somewhere in far off Germany,
Or far off Prague – then what the hell!
But behind a Soviet door,
And in a Soviet hotel!

I back off, narrow my eyes.
I do not open the door.
After all, I have been raised
In a different literature.

Aleksandr Kushner (translated by Daniel Weissbort)

The Door

Go and open the door.
  Maybe outside there's
  a tree, or a wood,
  a garden,
  or a magic city.

Go and open the door.
  Maybe a dog's rummaging.
  Maybe you'll see a face,
or an eye,
or the picture
          of a picture.

Go and open the door.
  If there's a fog
  it will clear.

Go and open the door.
  Even if there's only
  the darkness ticking,
  even if there's only
  the hollow wind,
  even if
      nothing
          is there,
go and open the door.

At least
there'll be
a draught.

Miroslav Holub
(translated by Ian Milner and George Theiner)

Cultural Directives

As Michelangelo, the great Italian composer,
once remarked: Artists have responsibilities.
Hearing music is like contracting a disease,
a beautiful infection. It brings closer
the point of no return. One must be strong.
There's no such creature as a harmless song.

Painting too, as the English artist Shakespeare
pointed out, can be debilitating
unless you aspire beyond paint to real things.
A painting freezes movement. The eye, like the ear,
is a channel of impotence. Mere airs and graces
often induce an unproductive stasis.

And as for words, I only need quote Mozart,
the Swiss poet: They're tainted by unreason.
Language is discourse, words slippery. To seize one
we must lay traps, as for mice. The throat's part
of the respiratory tract, and you may clip
a speech, like air, by tightening your grip.

Too many of you are wasting your time and ours
with gewgaws, bric-à-brac and frolicking.
It's time to give you all a rollocking.
We're not impressed, I fear, by your endeavours.
The role of the past is to prepare the future
and your task is to welcome it with Culture.

George Szirtes

The Burning of the Books

When the Regime commanded that books with harmful
knowledge
Should be publicly burned and on all sides
Oxen were forced to drag cartloads of books
To the bonfires, a banished
Writer, one of the best, scanning the list of the
Burned, was shocked to find that his
Books had been passed over. He rushed to his desk
On wings of wrath, and wrote a letter to those in power
Burn me! he wrote with flying pen, burn me! Haven't
my books
Always reported the truth? And here you are
Treating me like a liar! I command you:
Burn me!

Bertolt Brecht (translated by John Willett)

'This poem . . .'

This poem is dangerous: it should not be left
Within the reach of children, or even of adults
Who might swallow it whole, with possibly
Undesirable side-effects. If you come across
An unattended, unidentified poem
In a public place, do not attempt to tackle it
Yourself. Send it (preferably, in a sealed container)
To the nearest centre of learning, where it will be rendered
Harmless, by experts. Even the simplest poem
May destroy your immunity to human emotions.
All poems must carry a Government warning. Words
Can seriously affect your heart.

Elma Mitchell

Mayakovsky Square

The poets are burning
in Mayakovsky Square –
our tongues throw flames
into the night,
tease the uninformed police.
But we cannot be held responsible
for the drifting of leaves.

Disguised in strange hats
we evade their hammer eyes
or, street-wise, flee
through the city's back-yards.

In the camps we starve
and, in prison libraries
find our fathers –
Pushkin, Tolstoy, Lermentov,
untouched by fifty years' scouring.

Words do not fail us.

Liz Arden

In 1961 unofficial poetry readings were held in Mayakovsky Square, until their final suppression by the KGB.

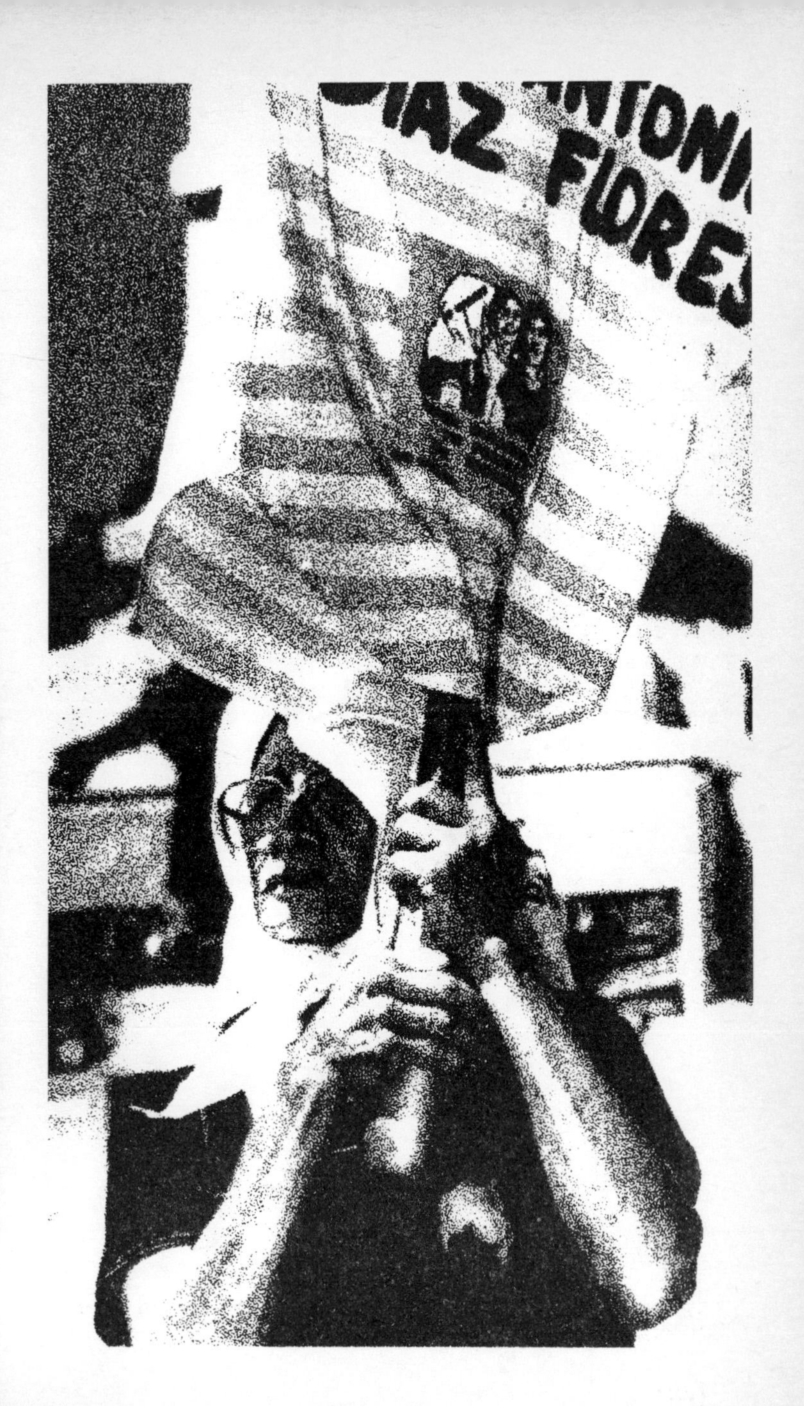
FLORES

I Shall Write

I shall write about all the sad people
Who have remained on the shore.
About those who have been condemned to silence –
I shall write.
Then burn what I have written.
Oh, how these lines will soar,
How the sheets of paper will fall back
Under the fierce blast
Of irreparable emptiness!
With what haughty movement
The fire will outstrip me!
And the ashen foam will tremble.
But give birth to nothing.

Irina Ratushinskaya
(translated by David McDuff)

Poet

for Irina Ratushinskaya

She lived for six years in a cage. When I
Am inclined to regret the way things are, I think
Of her who through long cold and pain did not
Betray the ones she loved or plead for mercy.
They censored the few letters they allowed.
Cabbage and bread, rotten and stale, were food.
While outside governments and springs went round
And summits, thaws, and great events occurred,
Here inside was no hope. Years of her youth
Were sickened for no crime. She did not even
Know if her lover knew she was alive.
The paper she'd written poems on was removed.
What could she find? – the swirls in the cold blue light
Through bars so thick her hands could not pass through
  them –
Those swirls of blue light and the heels of bread
She shared with some companionable mouse.
Her poems she memorized line by line and destroyed.
The Contents were what was difficult to remember.

Vikram Seth

A Mural in Mexico

Plain as a kick and straight to the eye.
On a consecrated wall we saw
your outstretched fists and a rising sun,
executed rapidly at midnight.

It is your substitute for a free press
and whitewash has already silenced it.
You know that has its uses, boys.
Until it flakes, government whitewash forms
a new canvas, generous in size, a page
for critical writing, satire and rage.

Martin Stokes

Poets: an Endangered Species

The death of Lorca worries me.
Why did they need to gun him down?

Not for being Red, or a *maricón*
but because he was a poet, and wrote poetry

in an iron age of civil war.
Mandelstam likewise.

He threw a squib in Stalin's eyes.
That wasn't what they killed him for:

his ironies of inner life
were insupportable by a state

built on fanaticism, hate,
suspicion. He knew well enough

to play the holy fool
in iron times was death:

he died each time he drew his breath.
What these learned in a harder school

than ours, we learn from history
that can't repeat itself as such

but doesn't scorn sequels overmuch.
The death of Lorca worries me.

R. J. Caldwell

maricón: homosexual

Letter to Kate

When imprisoned in 1979 for 'incitement and obstruction', i.e. for having been a founder member of Charter 77, Vaclav Havel was allowed to write one four-page letter to his wife, Olga (his only wife), under the following restrictions: no crossings out or corrections were allowed; no quotation marks, no underlinings or foreign expressions. 'We could only write about "family matters". Humour was banned as well: punishment is a serious business, after all, and jokes would have undermined the gravity.'

I reach for your name and then think
Better of it, but I'm not allowed
Crossings-out, so you must stand, my love.
Let me explain, not who I am –
For this being a family letter,
You must know me – but why you have been
Reacquainted with this lover. I am,
As they say, distanced from a more familiar
Kate – not her name, you understand –
And must not use life's mishap to deny
Things their consequences: you cannot recouple
For a jailor's convenience. Kate, the name,
Is less foreign than Medbh or Tracy; sufficiently
Far from earlier family and not likely
To be suspected as a joke. Dear Kate,
Though apart, we must thank our luck
To be living at the same time in history,
And as one of us is not attuned to jokes,
The ban on this right, sorry, rite (emphasized
Not underlined) is not, indeed, onerous.
There are games that we like, separately,
And by rehearsing play at times fixed
By some public clock – a cockerel crowing-in
The day, or a blackout where I live –
We might win safe conduct for this letter.
Or the next. Carnal matters I dare not
Hint at publicly. I should lose you then,
And be claimed by some professional wife
With your name. My love, I count your lashes –

Sorry, no private joke of bedrooms,
Just the miniature fans that frame your eyes;
And no hint, truly, of the days crossed off my back.

E. A. Markham

Sing a Song of Censorship

Sing a song of censorship, a pocketful of lies,
Four and twenty officers, each with eagle eyes,
Checking every column, forging every link –
Say thank you to the gentlemen who tell us what to think.

John Foster

Bunyan's Flute

The brutish clowns who run the world suppose
  That it is possible to silence song
  By locking up the singer. They are wrong.
  They think that clanking lock and key can close
In thought, can keep concepts at bay; that rows
  Of cells with iron bars can maim a strong
  Idea and make it yield. How long, how long
  Must this mad reasoning prevail? Who knows
What more injustices must be endured
  By those whose crime is that they thought and wrote?
  Bunyan in Bedford prison made a flute
Out of his stool's leg, played it while immured,
  Enraged his baffled jailers with its note
  Of pilgrim joy. Then let not me be mute.

Gerard Benson

'I shall'

I shall create
out of the darkness of my jail
my dawn
out of the jaws of hatred
my destiny.
I shall sing
the wind
the sun
the flowers
the spring.
I shall sing
in spite of fences
in spite of jailers
in spite of hatred.

Fouzi El-Asmar

'The day died'

The day died like a dog and won't come back,
So let's arrange a splendid funeral feast.
There will be many more days just as black,
I know. The further east
You go, the worse it gets
(That's the usual fate of pioneers!)
But evening's slow-paced gladness will revive
Our worn-out sinews like a healing spring.
The day is done. Our blood slows. We're alive,
Though life is harsh, the age unpitying.
We take another lovely draught, and let
The dusk carry us back to some lost place
Where, with our young audacity, we face
Freedom – and accept the price of it.

Irina Ratushinskaya
(translated by Carol Rumens)

from Acts, 22:28

And the chief captain answered,
With a great sum obtained I this freedom.
And Paul said, But I was free born.

(Authorized Version)

The poet Irina Ratushinskaya was arrested in September 1982 and from April 1983 to October 1986 was held in the Small Zone, a special unit for women prisoners of conscience in Barashevo, Mordovia. This poem was written in the Small Zone in March 1985.

Night Watch

Awake for hours and staring at the ceiling
Through the unsettled stillness of the night
He grows possessed of the obsessive feeling
That dawn has come and gone and brought no light.

Vikram Seth

Sonnet

The month of January has flown past
the prison windows; I have heard the singing
of convicts in their labyrinth of cells:
'One of our brothers has regained his freedom.'
You still can hear the prisoners' low song,
the echoing footsteps of the wordless wardens.
And you yourself still sing, sing silently:
'Farewell, o January.'
Facing the window's light,
you swallow the warm air in giant gulps.
But I roam once again, sunk deep in thought,
down hallways, from the last interrogation
to the next one – toward that distant land
where there is neither March nor February.

Joseph Brodsky (translated by George L. Kline)

A Political Prisoner Listening to a Cicada

While the year sinks westward,
  I hear a cicada
Bid me to be resolute here in my cell,
Yet it needed the beat of those black wings
To break a white-haired prisoner's heart . . .
His flight is heavy through the fog,
His pure voice drowns in the windy world.
Who knows if he be singing still?
Who listens to me any more?

Lo Pin Wang

Some Advice to Those Who Will Serve Time in Prison

. . . To wait for letters inside,
to sing sad songs,
or to lie awake all night staring at the ceiling
                    is sweet but dangerous.
Look at your face from shave to shave,
forget your age,
watch out for lice
                    and for spring nights,
            and always remember
                    to eat every last piece of bread –
also don't forget to laugh heartily.
   And who knows,
   the woman you love may stop loving you.
   Don't say it's no big thing:
   it's like the snapping of a green branch
                              to the man inside.
   To think of roses and gardens inside is bad,
   to think of seas and mountains is good.
   Read and write without rest,
   and I also advise weaving
   and making mirrors.
   I mean, it's not that you can't pass
            ten or fifteen years inside
                              and more –
              you can,
              as long as the jewel
              on the left side of your chest doesn't
              lose its lustre!

Nazim Hikmet

The poet Nazim Hikmet was held for eighteen years
as a political prisoner in Turkey.

from To Althea, From Prison

Stone walls do not a prison make,
  Nor iron bars a cage;
Minds innocent and quiet take
  That for an hermitage;
If I have freedom in my love,
  And in my soul am free;
Angels alone that soar above
  Enjoy such liberty.

Richard Lovelace (1618–1657)

Objectivity

On a dark night
Only when you turn the light out
in your room
Can you see beyond
the window pane.

Mahmood Jamal

Poem for a Political Prisoner

So many whispers. You're not here –
this is what I'm awake to.
I pretend there's nothing to fear.
So many whispers. You're not here.
These days, nothing is clear –
your voice keeps straining through
whispers. Love, you're not here –
this is what I'm awake to.

Katherine Gallagher

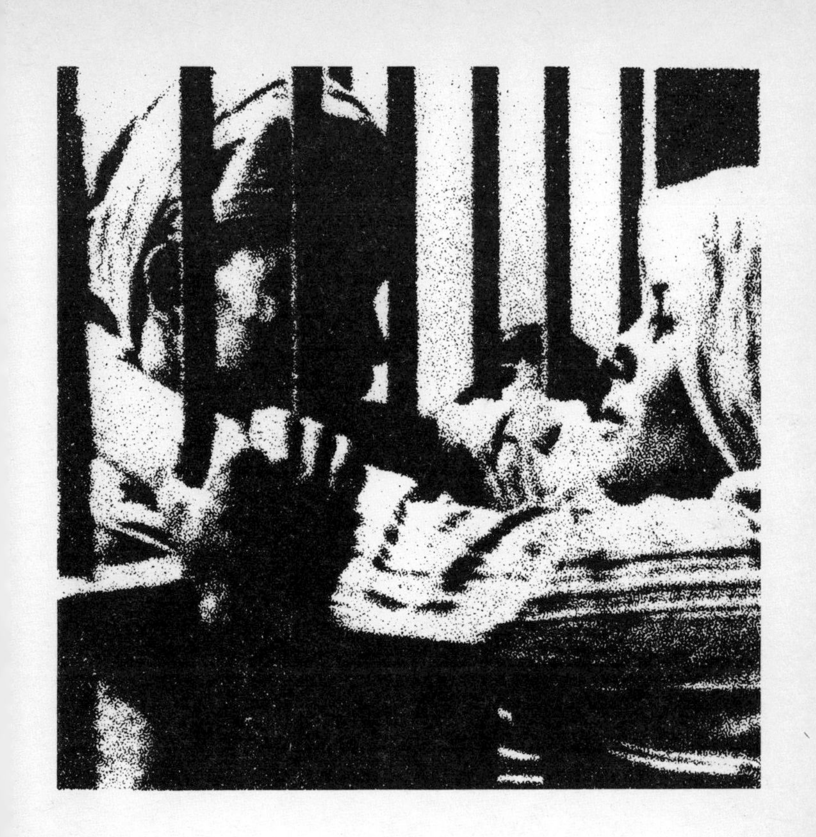

Replay

When asked how he spent
His blindfold years,
The released hostage said
He'd heard the sounds
And watched the pictures
That played in his head.

Favourite pieces of music,
Incidents recalled,
Their details so defined,
He began to question
What was real
And what was in his mind,

Though his greatest fear
Was finding one day
When he tried to switch it on,
That his mind was empty
And all the sounds
And all the pictures had gone.

When asked how he spent his time now,
The released hostage said
The worst times are when he's alone
With the pictures in his head.

Pat Moon

Farewell

Farewell to the bushy clump close to the river
And the flags where the butter-bump hides in for ever;
Farewell to the weedy nook, hemmed in by waters;
Farewell to the miller's brook and his three bonny
  daughters;
Farewell to them all while in prison I lie –
In the prison a thrall sees nought but the sky.

Shut out are the green fields and birds in the bushes;
In the prison yard nothing builds, blackbirds or thrushes.
Farewell to the old mill and dash of the waters,
To the miller and, dearer still, to his three bonny daughters.

In the nook, the large burdock grows near the green willow;
In the flood, round the moorcock dashes under the billow;
To the old mill farewell, to the lock, pens, and waters,
To the miller himsel', and his three bonny daughters.

John Clare (1793–1864)

From 1837 to 1841 John Clare was a voluntary patient at an asylum near Epping. After only five months at home he was removed to Northampton County Asylum where he stayed until his death in 1864 at the age of seventy. This poem was written during his confinement.

After Interrogation

Two strides forward, two across.
The floor is slippery with ice.
Stretch your arms, you touch the walls.
Raise your head, you strike the ceiling.

And yet out there are boundless fields,
Deep rivers plunged.
The mountains echoing,
The sky
Flapped by its bird wings,
And rushing far away,
The roads.

There's your vast-expanding native land.
There are also the friends you've loved,
The dreams you've cherished,
And at least a space,
Just two strides wide,
Where you stand up
For all of these.

Georgi Djagarov (translated by Theodore Weiss)

'The Life that tied too tight escapes'

The Life that tied too tight escapes
Will ever after run
With a prudential look behind
And spectres of the Rein –
The Horse that scents the living Grass
And sees the Pastures smile
Will be retaken with a shot
If he is caught at all –

Emily Dickinson (1830–1886)

The Hostages

A song for Elton John

Tara Tara Tara
Tara Tara Tara

They have taken the heroes from Tara
  and tucked them away in the Tain.
There are whins on the Rath of the Synods
  and the Kings are in Brugh na Boyne.

Tara Tara Tara

But here is the Mound of the Hostages.
  This is the Mound of the Hostages.
Where have they hidden the hostages
  who were the strength of Kings?

The shackles are rusted and broken.
  The hostages are gone.
They slept in the dark at Tara
  and woke in Lebanon.

Tara Tara Tara

The heroes have risen from Nemnagh,
  and the Kings from the river-bed.
They have sounded the horn for Keenan
  and the echoes roused the dead.

Tara Tara Tara

The heroes have risen from Nemnagh.
  The Kings are at the gate.
They have sounded the horn for McCarthy
  and Sutherland and Waite.

Tara Tara Tara

And here is the Mound of the Hostages.
  This is the Mound of the Hostages.
Where have they hidden the hostages
  who wore the chains of Kings?

In the dark they are speaking in whispers.
  They are fettered hand and foot.
But in front of the Mound there is open ground
  from Tara to Beirut.

Tara Tara Tara
Tara Tara Tara

Conor Carson (14)

from The Ballad of Reading Gaol

I know not whether Laws be right,
  Or whether Laws be wrong;
All that we know who lie in gaol
  Is that the wall is strong;
And that each day is like a year,
  A year whose days are long.

But this I know, that every Law
  That men have made for Man,
Since first Man took his brother's life,
  And the sad world began,
But straws the wheat and saves the chaff
  With a most evil fan.

This too I know – and wise it were
  If each could know the same –
That every prison that men build
  Is built with bricks of shame,
And bound with bars lest Christ should see
  How men their brothers maim.

With bars they blur the gracious moon,
  And blind the goodly sun:
And they do well to hide their Hell,
  For in it things are done
That Son of God nor son of Man
  Ever should look upon!

*   *   *

The vilest deeds like poison weeds
  Bloom well in prison-air:
It is only what is good in Man
  That wastes and withers there:
Pale Anguish keeps the heavy gate,
  And the Warder is Despair.

Oscar Wilde

Poem for the Executioners

This is a blinding-place.
Only the hangmen see
fixing the knot of shame
upon their chosen tree.

Moments of waiting shrill,
finally echo out
past the creak of startled wood
and a soon-muffled shout.

Slowly the air recoils
on another unheard plea
and light is locked upon
a desolate, marked tree.

Katherine Gallagher

Epitaph

They hanged him on a clement morning, swung
between the falling sunlight and the women's
breathing, like a black apostrophe to pain.
All morning while the children hushed
their hopscotch joy and the cane kept growing
he hung there sweet and low.
                    At least that's how
they tell it. It was long ago
and what can we recall of a dead slave or two
except that when we punctuate our island tale
they swing like sighs across the brutal
sentences, and anger pauses
till they pass away.

Dennis Scott

from The Mask of Anarchy

What art thou Freedom? O! could slaves
Answer from their living graves
This demand – tyrants would flee
Like a dream's dim imagery . . .

P. B. Shelley (1792–1822)

Height

The bird's long flown away
the flower has wilted
the rain is lost

Noontide is silently enveloped
in sunlit contemplation
The wind sweetly gathers
the forest scents

A stone has gently rolled
into the water

And after many centuries I saw
in its trembling
the rocking of
a distant shore.

Mateja Matevski (translated by Ewald Osers)

Unter den Linden

In Unter den Linden and Wenceslas Square
the candles wink their *laissez-faire*,
people are trampling over borders,
packing their luggage. Cassette recorders
hiss like steam in the cold air,

cameras roll and spokesmen prepare
brief noncommittal statements, tear
pages from notebooks and wait for orders.
Prisons open: prisoners and warders
  mix in Unter den Linden.

In Prague and Budapest they wear
rosettes, wave flags. A furious year
gathers to a close. The wind disorders
ships of state and fleets of boarders.
Men link hands, dance and boldly stare
  across Unter den Linden.

George Szirtes

Die Mauer ist Runter

The wall is down. Incredulous
we contemplate, through raw gateways,
dawn in the west. You, the baker,
me, the busdriver, there the student
carrying a flag, there the woman
who cannot forget or forgive –
we move through rubble,
through the searchlights,
through the watercannon's crazy rain.

This is the real dance;
we stitch its paces over the Kaiser's cobbles,
in between the Weimar tramlines,
through Hitler's broken archways, empty squares,
up and down the grim lattices
of Russian tanktracks.
Laughing, we invade the territory
inside each other's arms.
At such times worlds end and worlds begin.

Dick Jones

New Jeans

To our young East German tourist guide;
Potsdam, 1990

Long grasses wave,
Russian lorries pass.
Who killed whom
she didn't say,
only which architects
passed this way.

Jennie Milnes

Chinese White

Do you remember that scene in *Ashes and Diamonds* where
the hero rushes forward through the clotheslines and bleeds
to death among the sheets? Or was it
in *Canal* (I can't remember now). A square
of white turns slowly red. The redness fades
to black and white. The picture is a composite,

a form of poster. The War, the Resistance,
something about betrayal, all mixed up
in a child's mind who didn't see
the war, for whom it is a haunting presence
of sheets and blood. An image hangs and drops
in a grey passageway or alley.

His name was Zbigniew, and he wore dark glasses,
and later he jumped from a train (a true life fact)
because, well, Poles are like that,
they get drunk, morose, et cetera. The girl who kisses
the boy was blonde as always. Was it an act
of bravery him getting shot

or cowardice? We could look it up in books
but that is not the point (we pull our serious face)
but something in the falling, the how
and where of it. And so wherever one looks
the same old images return and find their place,
a square, an alleyway, a row

of ordinary houses suddenly still and hot
and people falling lying as if on a square
of film. You see the victim's head
as someone aims and shoots him, and you cut
to tanks or bodies or a sheet hung out to air,
a white square slowly turning red.

George Szirtes

In June 1989 the Chinese army moved with tanks into a peaceful pro-democracy demonstration being held in Tiananmen Square, Beijing. Amnesty International's preliminary findings after two months of extensive research reported over 1000 civilian deaths and many thousands wounded.

The Liberator

A Political Allegory

In the high trees – many doleful winds;
The ocean waters – lashed into waves.
If the sharp sword be not in your hand,
How can you hope your friends will remain many?
Do you not see that sparrow on the fence?
Seeing the hawk it casts itself into the snare.
The fowler to catch the sparrow is delighted;
The Young Man to see the sparrow is grieved.
He takes his sword and cuts through the netting;
The yellow sparrow flies away, away.
Away, away, up to the blue sky
And down again to thank the Young Man.

Ts'ao Chih (AD 192–232) (translated by Arthur Waley)

All You Who Sleep Tonight

All you who sleep tonight
Far from the ones you love,
No hand to left or right,
And emptiness above –

Know that you aren't alone.
The whole world shares your tears,
Some for two nights or one,
And some for all their years.

Vikram Seth

Christmas Day 1989

'We might as well be living in Rumania.'
– Reported remark by Queen Mary at the time of the Abdication Crisis, 1936

A dodgy ally, bad example,
The symptom of a tyrant's mania,
Concourse of nations' damaged sample,
A kind of botched-up Ruritania.

Time's elbow gives us all a nudge,
And sends us hurrying back to school as
We learn that we must never judge
A gallant people by its rulers.

James N. Dawson

The Coming of the Ice

For years we saw it far away,
The glitter of ice on the mountain tops;
For years heard the ringing
Night-cracks:

But we stayed on,
Hooking the huge rich fish
Out of the black deep.

Now it is all round us, the ice,
Mile upon groaning mile –
We shall be shards – sleek,

Warm as we are with gold oil –
Dry pressed,
After the terrible great gorging,
Suspended in crystal.

Vuyelwa Carlin

Eastern Europe: 1990

Ice-gripped we ached to be set free,
Knowing each year what winter meant –
Slow months of certain tyranny
And solid snow-imprisonment.

It's easier now not having to
Shovel grey slush or scrape grey frost
Off paths and windscreens, worrying though
That the old certainty's been lost.

No forecast warned how gales tear down
Some ageing tyrant-statue tree,
How banks collapse and cattle drown
In the quick floods of liberty.

Climatic changes come about
To test our knowing where we stand –
On water, when the ice thaws out?
And, when the flood subsides, dry land?

Robert Roberts

Frontiers

At this point there's no reason not to cross.
Here, in the hills, border patrols are few,
No powerful glasses sweep from the nearby Schloss,
The river that severs in the plain is too
Shallow to more than inconvenience
And a cripple could hop across the one-bar fence.

Admittedly in such a time and place
There's not much to be said for changing sides.
The world on either side wears the same face
And who's to mark the differences it hides;
And voices heard across the fence or stream
Appear to be talking about a similar dream.

But when the weather changes or one walks
Up to the village or down to where the land
Spreads out below the hills, or when one talks
Not of the dream but of what's really planned;
It's then one judges the leap or tries to order
The pattern of patrols along the border.

The thing to do at that stage is stand still
Screened by bushes, hidden behind a tree
On the stream's bank and gaze around until
You've absorbed the narrow scene, then you might see
Among the cover on the other side
Another watcher trying to decide.

W. M. Tidmarsh

Visa for a Return Visit Refused

An official in Prague tosses a pin into the air;
a small rusty pin, slightly bent, and it lands on NO;
and *no* he cables back to my supplication for a visa.

The trees of Bohemia fall into line and march away;
further and further they recede and smaller and darker,
a distancing army of ants; then snow; a blankness of snow.

Gerda Mayer

'These Strangers, in a foreign World'

These Strangers, in a foreign World,
Protection asked of me –
Befriend them, lest Yourself in Heaven
Be found a Refugee –

Emily Dickinson

In Fields As They Lay

We're working in the Church today.
Crib. Manger. Straw and beast.
The family and their place to stay.
The warm familiar Christmas Feast.

But then we hear distasteful news:
Our quaint village, 'Best Kept' (Nineteen
Eighty four), twinned with Lyndt, charming views,
Has hippy folk on the village green.

Grubby children whoop in the rain,
Shaven heads and sheepskins appear,
A ragged tent, rough dog on a chain:
Travellers. Why *now*? Why *here*?

We observe, and for a while
A whiff of wilderness invades,
Writ in their skins, their eyes, their style,
The hallmarks of survival's trades.

Living in the world's draught, damp as mould,
They must surely trust as we have ceased
To trust and hunger in December cold.
What passes for a star in their East?

We'll not see them for long. We've sent
Police and bailiff up the lane
To pack their bags and kids and tent
And get them on their way again.

Ah, we've worked in the Church all day,
Now midnight carols resound in glory.
No strangers looking for a place to stay
Will spoil our cosy Christmas story.

Rowland Molony

On Exiles and Defeats

No. It was not the bad time in Chena,
nor the sudden grim prosecutions
in improvised war councils.
No. The blind gun that hit me on the shoulder
didn't defeat me,
nor investigation's black hood of horror
nor the grey hell of the stadiums
with their roars of terror.

No. Neither was it the iron bars at the window
cutting us in pieces from life,
nor the watch kept on our house
nor the stealthy tread,
nor the slide into the deep maw of hunger.

No. What defeated me was the street that was not mine,
the borrowed language learned in hastily set-up courses.
What defeated me was the lonely, uncertain figure
in longitudes that did not belong to us.
It was Greenwich
longitude zero
close to nothing.

What defeated me was the alien rain,
forgetting words
the groping memory,
friends far away
and the atrocious ocean between us,
wetting the letters I waited for
which did not come.

What defeated me was yearning day after day
at Jerningham Road
agonising under the fog
at Elephant and Castle
sobbing on London Bridge.

And I was defeated step by step
by the harsh calendar;
and between Lunes-Monday and Martes-Tuesday
I had shrivelled into a stranger.

What defeated me was the absence of your tenderness, my
country.

Maria Eugenia Bravo (translated by Cicely Herbert)

Sage

If you are slightly bored, you are in luck,
and should not ask the gods to organise
too long an outing from the days you dwell in;
such prayers have a knack of being heard,
and exile is a hard land to do well in.

The guru spoke – and from experience.
And yawned. And wished himself ten bolts of
thunder hence.

Gerda Mayer

Pendulum

The nervous mother shouting ceaselessly
At her roped children swinging from the tree
Remembers with a start she once was young
And terrified her mother as she swung.

Vikram Seth

The Grass Speaks

Yes: I shall lift this stone
though you may set
demons with double skill
to retch and sweat
gouging the naked rock . . .
leave it to me.
Soon, while the seasons pass,
gradually
I will uplift this stone
shifting its weight
with slow persistence as
early and late
my green blade, thin as flame,
chisels a way
through the soil's thickest night.
Although men say
time is a healer
I wound as I come
breaking earth's silvered skin.
Though I am dumb
infinite powers
are harnessed in me.
Yes: I shall lift this stone.
Wait. You will see.

Jean Kenward

The Mouse that Gnawed the Oak-Tree Down

The mouse that gnawed the oak-tree down
Began his task in early life.
He kept so busy with his teeth
He had no time to take a wife.

He gnawed and gnawed through sun and rain
When the ambitious fit was on,
Then rested in the sawdust till
A month of idleness had gone.

He did not move about to hunt
The coteries of mousie-men.
He was a snail-paced, stupid thing
Until he cared to gnaw again.

The mouse that gnawed the oak-tree down,
When that tough foe was at his feet –
Found in the stump no angel-cake
Nor buttered bread, nor cheese nor meat –

The forest-roof let in the sky.
'This light is worth the work,' said he.
'I'll make this ancient swamp more light,'
And started on another tree.

Vachel Lindsay

To Toussaint l'Ouverture

Toussaint, the most unhappy man of men!
Whether the whistling Rustic tend his plough
Within thy hearing, or thy head be now
Pillowed in some deep dungeon's earless den; –
O miserable Chieftain! where and when
Wilt thou find patience! Yet die not; do thou
Wear rather in thy bonds a cheerful brow:
Though fallen thyself, never to rise again,
Live, and take comfort. Thou has left behind
Powers that will work for thee; air, earth, and skies;
There's not a breathing of the common wind
That will forget thee; thou hast great allies;
Thy friends are exultations, agonies,
And love, and man's unconquerable mind.

William Wordsworth (1770–1850)

Toussaint l'Ouverture led the Negro slaves in Haiti against their French masters at the time of the French Revolution. He drove out the French, but they later seized him after asking him to a meeting to discuss peace; he died in a dungeon in France.

A Vision

I lost the love of heaven above,
  I spurned the lust of earth below,
I felt the sweets of fancied love,
  And hell itself my only foe.

I lost earth's joys, but felt the glow
  Of heaven's flame abound in me,
Till loveliness and I did grow
  The bard of immortality.

I loved but woman fell away,
  I hid me from her faded fame,
I snatch'd the sun's eternal ray
  And wrote till earth was but a name.

In every language upon earth,
  On every shore, o'er every sea,
I gave my name immortal birth
  And kept my spirit with the free.

John Clare

Evening in Ahungalle

The sun smoulders,
a giant wheel in the sky;
the sand strikes cinder sparks
as we bathe listless feet or lie

around the rocky coves: heat-soaked,
we watch the perambulating gulls
swoop in semicircular abandon.
A dry breeze evolves

to comfort us. The Swedes, Celts,
Angles/Saxons disrobe:
sun worshippers from affluent lands.
We do not probe

these particular rites; instead we
sell ourselves, the sea, the endless sand.
The sky replies, darkening in resonance.
The evening descends with heavy hand.

A year later the land is fractured.
In the water young bones lie in shreds
Like splintered wood; her skin
of burnished gold is bleached dry.

Yvonne Gunawardena

This poem was written in memory of all the young men and women who have lost their lives in the violence in Sri Lanka.

Against the Storm

War gathers again and the stern
Generals argue over outspread maps.
Bullets shatter the high
Pulpit where a prelate pleads.
Ministers rant on platforms until
Words discard meaning and collapse.
Everywhere unease spreads like rumour.

Before it was the same, and small
Signals went unnoticed in the dark.
The gross cloud changed nothing despite
The thronged chambers, the skin
Shed like a stocking in the bomb's wake.
Afterwards, the cafes opened and stark
Lessons were unlearned. Unreal and loud,
Laughter drowned the warnings calling

Urgent as the cry of a trapped hare.
In spite of headlines now I catch
The stir of my sleeping son
Turning to begin his second year.
Against all horror I set such acts,
Intimate and warm as gathered friends
Huddled in a room against the storm
Or around the table for a final meal.

Sean Dunne

This was written after the killing of Archbishop Romero in 1980. Archbishop Romero, a champion of economic and social reforms in El Salvador and vocal critic of both left- and right-wing extremists, was shot whilst saying mass for his dead mother at the high altar.

Marie Wilson

Enniskillen

Under the statue
  of the Unknown Soldier
a man prepares
  a bomb. He is
an unknown soldier.

The patron saint of warriors
  is Michael.
Between the unknown soldiers
  is a wall.
It is the gable
  of St Michael's Hall.

This was Remembrance Sunday.
  Poppy Day.
They came to hear
  the bugles in the Square.
They did not count
  the unknown soldiers there.

Today there were no sermons.
  Unknown soldiers
said later it had not
  gone off as planned.
Under the bricks
  she held her father's hand.

Today there was no Last Post.
  Her last words
were 'Daddy, I love you.'
  He said he would trust
God. But her poppy
  lay in the dust.

The protector of unknown soldiers
  is Michael.
The father is at the grave.
  A bell peals.
The name Michael
  means 'God Heals'.

Conor Carson [14]

Service

For X, in service,
    probably not lovely,
        no-one's daughter
            in particular,

who lost her hours
    of daylight on her knees
        to a gritstone floor,
            never raising her eyes

but to climb to an attic
    by a back stair, glad
        of a share of a mattress,
            too knackered to dream . . .

for her, and all the others,
    this:
        the old scullery floor
            is cracking up.

A flagstone
    four men could not lift
        has buckled and split.
            A hundred years

it's taken it, but look,
    a mushroom!
        Pale white skin
            as soft as yours.

This is her flesh,
    a musty taste
        of earth, but sweet.
            In memory of X . . .

take, eat.

Philip Gross

And Death Shall Have No Dominion

And death shall have no dominion.
Dead men naked they shall be one
With the man in the wind and the west moon;
When their bones are picked clean and the clean bones gone,
They shall have stars at elbow and foot;
Though they go mad they shall be sane,
Though they sink through the sea they shall rise again;
Though lovers be lost love shall not;
And death shall have no dominion.

And death shall have no dominion.
Under the windings of the sea
They lying long shall not die windily;
Twisting on racks when sinews give way,
Strapped to a wheel, yet they shall not break;
Faith in their hands shall snap in two,
And the unicorn evils run them through;
Split all ends up they shan't crack;
And death shall have no dominion.

And death shall have no dominion.
No more may gulls cry at their ears
Or waves break loud on the seashores;
Where blew a flower may a flower no more
Lift its head to the blows of the rain;
Though they be mad and dead as nails,
Heads of the characters hammer through daisies;
Break in the sun till the sun breaks down,
And death shall have no dominion.

Dylan Thomas

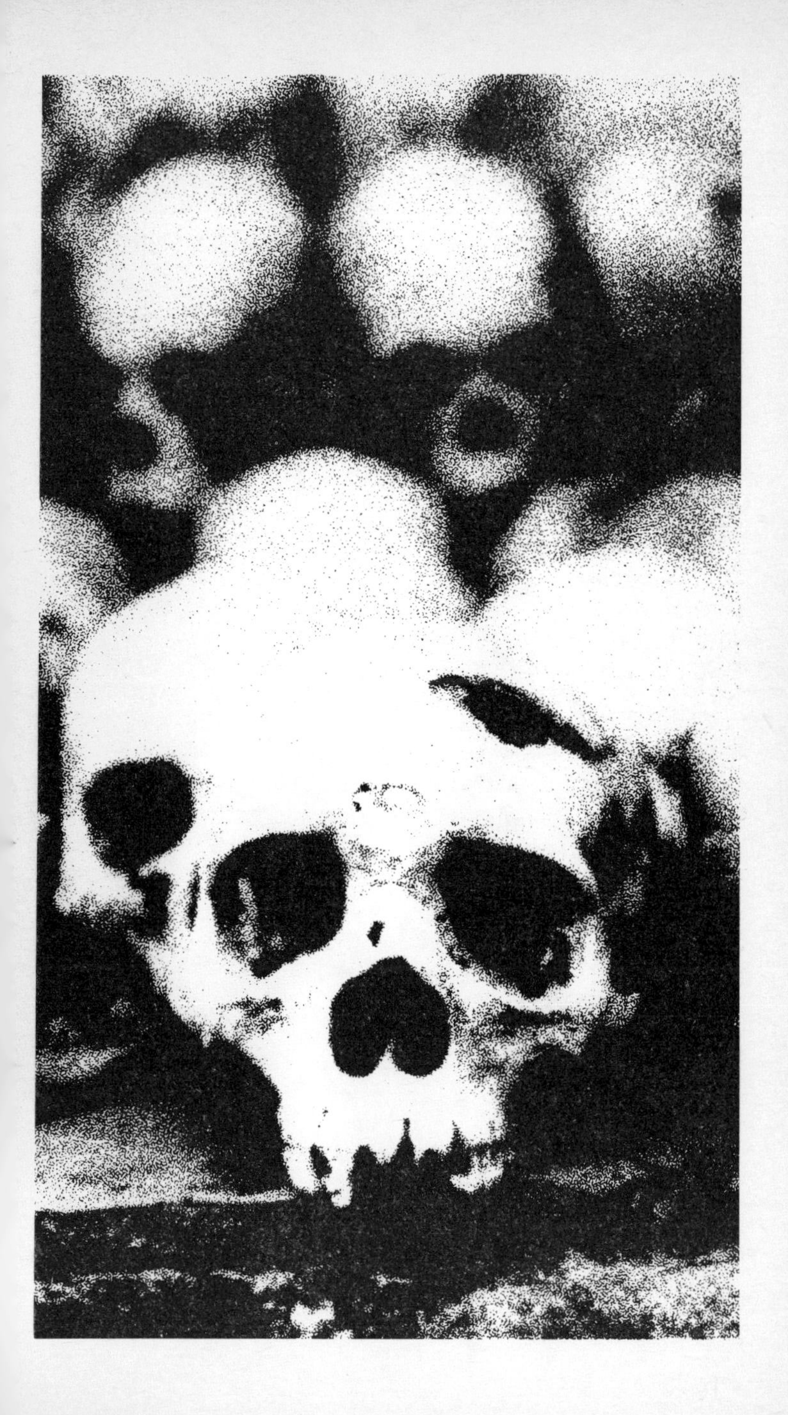

'No Rack can torture me'

No Rack can torture me –
My Soul – at Liberty –
Behind this mortal Bone
There knits a bolder One –

You cannot prick with saw –
Nor pierce with Scimitar –
Two Bodies – therefore be –
Bind One – The Other fly –

The Eagle of his Nest
No easier divest –
And gain the Sky
Than mayest Thou –

Except Thyself may be
Thine Enemy –
Captivity is Consciousness –
So's Liberty.

Emily Dickinson

Political Prisoners

(for Nelson Mandela and Bram Fischer)

They call from behind
the wires.

It's still the same message
fenced-off

and their truth floats
upwards. You can see it,

a kite held high, suspended
where nothing particular

is happening.
But they keep holding it

before the eyes
of their jailers

and it sails all winds
in a tiny patch of sky.

Katherine Gallagher

'No Prisoner be'

No Prisoner be –
Where Liberty –
Himself – abide with Thee –

Emily Dickinson

Determination

Whip me
Fetch more whips
  more executioners
  by the thousands
Turn my skin
into shoe soles
Rub salt in every wound
old wounds
new wounds
Search my mind
for every thread of a new image
of a new poem,
Take away the pen and the pencil.
With my blood
I shall write
every day
a million songs.

Fouzi El-Asmar

Celebration

(for Nizametdin Akhmetov)

He stood at the rostrum
filling the hall with words like 'love',
'freedom' and 'forgiveness':
they crisscrossed –
bunched, thrown into the air.

Prisoner at nineteen, thirty-nine now,
he was a freed man uncurling his tongue,
words finally his to speak. Earlier he'd
shipped them out hidden in logs (his poems
that will not lie down); they beat their way,
stern fingers tapping. Through holes in his voice
he told of days in a mental hospital –
legs swollen from beatings,
his wondering if they might be amputated
from lack of medical care.

No one in the hall could reach him.
He was the eyes of a man seeing spring
differently. He thanked his liberators,
praised newness, daffodils through the window.
'You don't know how I longed for this,' he said.

Katherine Gallagher

Thanks to pressure from P.E.N. in particular, Nizametdin Akhmetov was freed – one of the first 'glasnost' dissidents to be let go.

Where the Mind is Without Fear

Where the mind is without fear and the head is
  held high;
Where knowledge is free;
Where the world has not been broken up into
  fragments by narrow domestic walls;
Where words come out from the depth of
  truth;
Where tireless striving stretches its arms towards
  perfection;
Where the clear stream of reason has not lost
  its way into the dreary desert sand of dead
  habit;
Where the mind is lead forward by thee into
  ever-widening thought and action –
Into that heaven of freedom, my Father, let
  my country awake.

Rabindranath Tagore

'Come all!'

Come all! Stand up!
Just over there the dawn is coming.
Now I hear
Soft laughter.

Anon (Papago Indian)

Hamra Night

A candle in a long street
A candle in the sleep of houses
A candle for frightened shops
A candle for bakeries
A candle for a journalist trembling in an empty office
A candle for a fighter
A candle for a woman doctor watching over patients
A candle for the wounded
A candle for plain talk
A candle for the stairs
A candle for a hotel packed with refugees
A candle for a singer
A candle for broadcasters in their hideouts
A candle for a bottle of water
A candle for the air
A candle for two lovers in a naked flat
A candle for the falling sky
A candle for the beginning
A candle for the ending
A candle for the last communiqué
A candle for conscience
A candle in my hands.

Sa'di Yusuf (translated by Abdullah al-Udhari)

Hamra: a fashionable district in Beirut

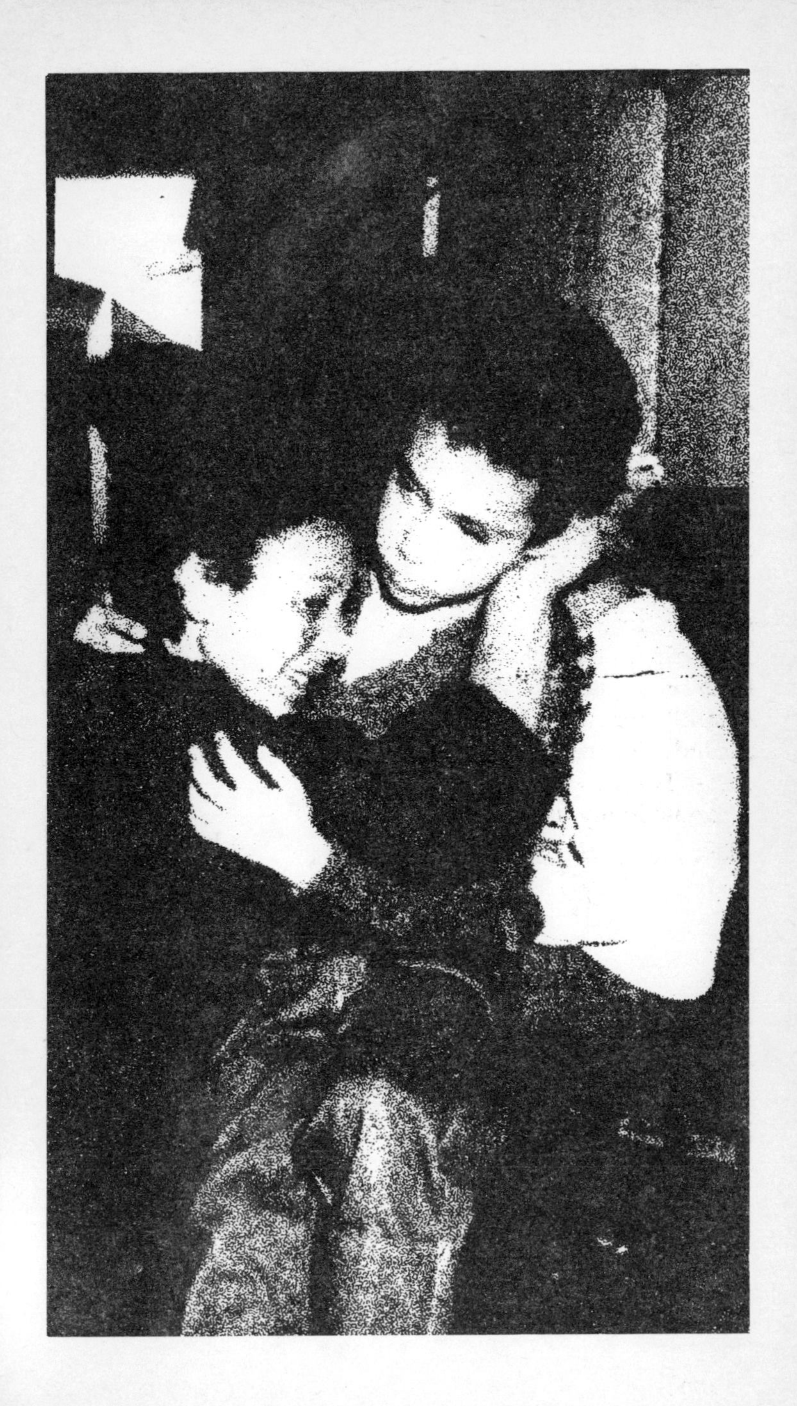

Acknowledgements

I would like to express special thanks to all the poets who have contributed to this book, many of whom have also donated their own fees to Amnesty International. Special thanks also to my husband – who paid the mortgage while I did it!

For permission to reprint the poems in this anthology the editor and publishers gratefully acknowledge the following:

Liz Arden: 'Mayakovsky Square', © Liz Arden, 1991, reprinted by permission of the author.

W. H. Auden: 'The Unknown Citizen', from *Another Time* by W. H. Auden, reprinted by permission of Faber and Faber Ltd.

Gerard Benson: 'Bunyan's Flute', © Gerard Benson, 1991, reprinted by permission of the author.

Anon, Papago Indian: 'Come All!', from *In the Trail of the Wind* by John Bierhorst, © John Bierhorst, 1971. Reprinted by permission of Farrar, Straus & Giroux Inc.

Maria Eugenia Bravo: 'On Exiles and Defeats', © Maria Eugenia Bravo, 1988, transl. © Cicely Herbert, 1988. From Anthology of Latin American Poets in London, Latin American Writers Group, reprinted by permission of the author and translator.

Ann Bonner: 'The Ideal State', © Ann Bonner, 1991, reprinted by permission of the author.

Bertolt Brecht: 'The Democratic Judge', transl. Michael Hamburger, and 'The Burning of the Books', transl. John Willett from *Poems 1913–1956* by Bertolt Brecht, Methuen, reprinted by permission of Methuen, London.

Joseph Brodsky: 'Sonnet: The month of January has flown past', from *Joseph Brodsky: Selected Poems*, transl. George L. Kline, Penguin, 1973, transl. © George L. Kline, 1973; reproduced by permission of Penguin Books Ltd.

Michael Brophy: 'Guns for the Boys', © Michael Brophy, 1991, reprinted by permission of the author.

R. J. Caldwell: 'Poets: an Endangered Species', © R. J. Caldwell, 1991, reprinted by permission of the author.

Vuyelwa Carlin: 'The Coming of the Ice', first appeared in *Poetry Wales*, © Vuyelwa Carlin, 1988, reprinted by permission of the author.

Conor Carson: 'The Hostages' and 'Marie Wilson', © Conor Carson, Shell Young Poet of the Year 1990, reprinted by permission of the author.

Mevlut Ceylan: 'Open Your Arms', © Mevlut Ceylan, 1991. First published in *Chapman*, Spring 1987, reprinted by permission of the author.

Wang Chi: 'Tell Me Now' and Ts'ao Chih: 'The Liberator', both transl. Arthur Waley, from *Chinese Poems* by Arthur Waley, Unwin Hyman Ltd, reprinted by permission of HarperCollins Publishers.

James N. Dawson: 'Christmas Day 1989', © James N. Dawson, 1991, reprinted by permission of the author.

Georgi Djagarov: 'After Interrogation', © Georgi Djagarov, transl. © Theodore Weiss, from *Poets of Bulgaria*, ed. W. Meredith, Forest Books, reprinted by permission of Forest Books and Theodore Weiss.
Sean Dunne: 'Against the Storm', © Sean Dunne, 1991, reprinted by permission of the author.

Fouzi El-Asmar: 'I shall' and 'Determination', from *The Wind-Driven Reed*, Three Continents Press, Inc., © Fouzi El-Asmar, reprinted by permission of the author and Three Continents Press, Washington DC.
D. J. Enright: 'The Rebel', © D. J. Enright, 1974, from *Rhyme Times Rhyme*, Chatto & Windus, reprinted by permission of the author.

John Foster: 'Sing a Song of Censorship', © John Foster, 1991, reprinted by permission of the author.
Robert Frost: 'Not Quite Social', from *The Poetry of Robert Frost*, ed. Edward Connery Lathem, Jonathan Cape Ltd. Reprinted by permission of The Estate of Robert Frost and the Random Century Group Ltd.

Katherine Gallagher: 'Poem for a Political Prisoner' and 'Celebration', © Katherine Gallagher, 1991, reprinted by permission of the author. 'Poem for the Executioners' and 'Political Prisoners', © Katherine Gallagher, 1991, from *Fish-Rings on Water*, Forest Books. Reprinted by permission of Forest Books and the author.
Philip Gross: 'History Lesson', © Philip Gross, 1991, reprinted by permission of the author. 'Service', from *Manifold Manor* by Philip Gross, Faber and Faber, reprinted by permission of the author and Faber and Faber Ltd.
Yvonne Gunawardena: 'Evening in Ahungalle', © Yvonne Gunawardena, 1991, reprinted by permission of the author.

Seamus Heaney: 'A Constable Calls', from *Selected Poems* by Seamus Heaney, Faber and Faber, reprinted by permission of the author and Faber and Faber Ltd.
David Heidenstam: 'Domestic Policy', © David Heidenstam, 1991, reprinted by permission of the author.
Helen Heslop: 'Britons Never Shall Be Slaves', © Helen Heslop, 1991, reprinted by permission of the author.
Elizabeth Hillman: 'The Election', © Elizabeth Hillman, 1991, reprinted by permission of the author.
Miroslav Holub: 'The Door', © Miroslav Holub, 1967, from *Selected Poems* by Miroslav Holub, transl. Ian Milner, Penguin Books, 1967. Transl. © Penguin Books, 1967; reprinted by permission of Penguin Books Ltd.

Mahmood Jamal: 'Objectivity', © Mahmood Jamal, 1989, first pub. in *Life Doesn't Frighten Me At All*, comp. John Agard, Heinemann, 1989. Reprinted by permission of the author.
Dick Jones: 'Die Mauer ist Runter', © Dick Jones, 1991, reprinted by permission of the author.

Jean Kenward: 'The Grass Speaks', © Jean Kenward, 1991, reprinted by permission of the author.
Aleksandr Kushner: 'In the Hotel', from *Post-War Russian Poetry*, ed. D. Weissbort, Penguin Books Ltd, 1974. Transl. © Daniel Weissbort, reprinted by permission of Daniel Weissbort.

Philip Larkin: 'Homage to a Government', from *High Windows* by Philip Larkin, Faber and Faber, reprinted by permission of Faber and Faber Ltd.

E. A. Markham: 'Letter to Kate', © E. A. Markham, 1989, from *Hinterland*, comp. E. A. Markham, Bloodaxe. Reprinted by permission of the author.
Mateja Matevski: 'Height', © Mateja Matevski, transl. © Ewald Osers, from *Footprints of the Wind* by Mateja Matevski, transl. Ewald Osers, Forest Books, 1988. Reprinted by permission of Forest Books and Ewald Osers.
Gerda Mayer: 'Visa for a Return Visit Refused', © Gerda Mayer, 1983, from *A Heartache of Grass*, Peterloo Poets, 1988. (First pub. in *Poetry Durham*, 1983.) Reprinted by permission of Peterloo Poets and the author. 'Sage', © Gerda Mayer, 1976, from *The Knockabout Show*, Chatto & Windus, 1978. (First pub. *Gallery*, 1976.)
Phyllis McGinley: 'The Angry Man', from *The Love Letters of Phyllis McGinley*, reprinted by permission of the proprietors, Viking Penguin, Inc.
Robin Mellor: 'Thoughts in the Park', © Robin Mellor, 1991, reprinted by permission of the author.
Jennie Milnes: 'New Jeans', © Jennie Milnes, 1991, reprinted by permission of the author.
Elma Mitchell: 'The Watch-Dogs' and 'This Poem', © Elma Mitchell, 1987, from *People Etcetera: Poems New and Selected* by Elma Mitchell, Peterloo Poets, 1987. Reprinted by permission of Peterloo Poets and the author.
Rowland Molony: 'In Fields As They Lay', © Rowland Molony, 1991, reprinted by permission of the author.
Pat Moon: 'Replay', © Pat Moon, 1991, reprinted by permission of the author.

Grace Nichols: 'Two Old Black Men on a Leicester Square Park Bench', © Grace Nichols, reprinted by permission of the author.

Bulat Okudzhava: 'Ballad of the Paper Soldier', transl. Richard McKane, from *20th Century Russian Poetry*, Kozmik Press, reprinted by permission of Kozmik Press.

Irina Ratushinskaya: 'I Shall Write', from *No, I'm Not Afraid* by Irina Ratushinskaya, Bloodaxe, © Irina Ratushinskaya, transl. © David McDuff, reprinted by permission of the author and Bloodaxe Books. 'The Day Died', from *Pencil Letter* by Irina Ratushinskaya, Bloodaxe, © Irina Ratushinskaya, transl. © Carol Rumens, reprinted by permission of the author and Bloodaxe Books.

Robert Roberts: 'Eastern Europe: 1990', © Robert Roberts, 1991, reprinted by permission of the author.

Dennis Scott: 'Epitaph', © Dennis Scott, 1973, reprinted from *Uncle Time* by permission of The University of Pittsburgh Press.

Vikram Seth: 'Poet', 'Night Watch', 'All You Who Sleep Tonight' and 'Pendulum', from *All You Who Sleep Tonight* by Vikram Seth, Faber and Faber, 1990, reprinted by permission of Faber and Faber Ltd.

Tony Sims: 'Decree' and 'Voice of Authority', © Tony Sims, 1991, reprinted by permission of the author.

Martin Stokes: 'A Mural in Mexico', © Martin Stokes, 1991, reprinted by permission of the author.

George Szirtes: 'Cultural Directives', 'Unter den Linden' and 'Chinese White', © George Szirtes, 1991, reprinted by permission of the author.

Grete Tatler: 'Didactica Nova' and Daniela Crăsnaru: 'Everything is for our own good', from *Silent Voices*, transl. Andrea Deletant and Brenda Walker, Forest Books, 1986. Reprinted by permission of Forest Books.

Dylan Thomas: 'The Hand that Signed the Paper' and 'And Death Shall Have No Dominion', from *Collected Poems* by Dylan Thomas, Dent, reprinted by permission of David Higham Associates.

W. M. Tidmarsh: 'Frontiers', © W. M. Tidmarsh, 1978, reprinted by permission of the author.

Ruthven Todd: 'Dictator', from *Garland for the Winter Solstice*, Dent, reprinted by permission of David Higham Associates.

Kit Wright: 'Council of the Gods', © Kit Wright, reprinted by permission of the author.

Sa'di Yusuf: 'Hamra Night', from *Modern Poetry of the Arab World*, transl. Abdullah al-Udhari, Penguin Books, 1986, transl. © Abdullah al-Udhari, 1986; reprinted by permission of Penguin Books Ltd.

Faber and Faber Limited apologizes for any errors or omissions in the above list and would be grateful to be notified of any corrections that should be incorporated in the next edition of this volume.

End-note
About Amnesty International

Amnesty International is a worldwide movement independent of any government, political faction, ideology, economic interest, or religious creed. It seeks the release of prisoners of conscience: men and women detained anywhere for their beliefs, colour, sex, ethnic origin, language or religion who have neither used nor advocated violence. It advocates fair and early trials for all political prisoners and works on behalf of such people detained without charge or without trial. It opposes the death penalty and torture or other cruel, inhuman or degrading treatment or punishment of all prisoners. Amnesty International was awarded the Nobel Peace Prize in 1977 and the United Nations Human Rights Prize in 1978. If you would like further information or feel you can offer support in any way, please write to *Amnesty International British Section, 99–119 Rosebery Avenue, London* EC1R *4RE.*